MONEY

Fund-raising

Julie Haydon

A⁺

Smart Apple Media

This edition first published in 2006 in the United States of America by Smart Apple Media.

Smart Apple Media
2140 Howard Drive West
North Mankato
Minnesota 56003

First published in 2006 by
MACMILLAN EDUCATION AUSTRALIA PTY LTD
627 Chapel Street, South Yarra, Australia 3141

Visit our Web site at www.macmillan.com.au

Associated companies and representatives throughout the world.

Library of Congress Cataloging-in-Publication Data

Haydon, Julie.
  Fundraising / by Julie Haydon.
    p. cm — (Money)
  ISBN-13: 978-1-58340-785-1
  1. Fund raising—Juvenile literature. 2. Money-making projects for children—Juvenile literature. I. Title.
  II. Money (Smart Apple Media)

HG177.H394 2006
658.15'224—dc22   2005056797

Edited by Miriana Dasovic
Text and cover design by Raul Diche
Page layout by Raul Diche
Photo research by Legend Images
Illustrations by Ann Likhovetsky

Printed in USA

Acknowledgments
The author wishes to thank the Australian Red Cross.

The author and the publisher are grateful to the following for permission to reproduce copyright material:

Cover photograph: Children fundraising, courtesy of Photodisc; background image courtesy of Photodisc.

Coo-ee Picture Library, p. 10; Getty Images, p. 13; Frederick M. Brown/Getty Images, p. 14; © Greenpeace 2004, p. 18; iStock, pp 3, 32; Médecins Sans Frontières Australia, pp. 4, 15; Newspix, pp. 5, 6, 12, 19; Newspix, photo by Gary Graham, p. 17; Photodisc, pp. 7, 8; Photolibrary/Oxford Scientific Films, p. 21; Photolibrary/Picture Press, p. 20; Red Cross, pp. 26, 28; Red Cross/T Mayer, p. 29; RSPCA Victoria, pp. 22, 23, 24, 25; Save the Children Australia, pp. 11, 16; US Navy, p. 27; WSPA, p. 9.

While every care has been taken to trace and acknowledge copyright, the publisher tenders their apologies for any accidental infringement where copyright has proved untraceable. Where the attempt has been unsuccessful, the publisher welcomes information that would redress the situation.

Contents

Glossary words

When a word is printed in **bold**, you can look up its meaning in the glossary on page 31.

What is fund-raising?

Fund-raising is collecting money, or raising funds, for a charity, **cause**, event, or project. Money is collected from individuals, clubs, businesses, and governments. The money is used to improve the lives of people and animals.

Helping people and animals in need

Sometimes funds are raised to help people and animals in direct need. People and animals in direct need lack basic items, such as food and water. Sometimes they are injured or sick, or do not have anywhere to live. The money raised is used to help them become safe, healthy, and happy.

Charities sometimes raise funds to buy food and medicine, which they transport to those in need.

Info-plus!

- The Red Cross is an international charity that works in places where help is needed.
- Save the Whales is a cause working to stop the killing of whales.
- A school play is an event.
- Building a playground in a local park is a project.

Improving lives

Sometimes, fund-raising is used to improve the lives of people and animals who are not in direct need. People may raise money to plant trees in a park, or to send a music student on a study trip overseas. Money could be raised to build a new church or temple, or to build a skateboard ramp in a local park.

Raising money

Some fund-raising **campaigns** raise millions of dollars, while other campaigns raise less than a hundred dollars. The amount of money raised usually depends on:

- how big the campaign is. More people will hear about a big international campaign than a small local one

- why the money is being collected. More people may give **donations** to help people or animals in direct need than to help improve the lives of those who are not in direct need. People are also more likely to support campaigns they believe in

A woman sells drinks as part of a fund-raising campaign.

5

Sharing wealth

Fund-raising is one way of sharing wealth. Some people, communities, and countries are wealthier than others. By donating money, the wealthy can help those who do not have as much. **Volunteers** help by donating their time.

Everyone deserves to live a good life. People's basic needs, such as food, water, and shelter, should be met. They should be able to live in peace, not war. People should have the freedom to live the life they choose. Unfortunately, this does not always happen. Sharing wealth is not the answer to all problems, but it can help many people to have a better life.

Helping others

Many people want to help others but do not know how to, or do not have the time to help. By donating to a charity, cause, event, or project, people are able to help others simply and easily. Making donations can also make people feel good about themselves. They know that sharing their wealth will make a difference in other people's lives.

These children are collecting donations for music equipment for their school.

Products and services

Many people donate money during fund-raising campaigns, but some people donate **products** and **services** instead. These products and services may go directly to places where they can be used, or they may be sold to raise money for the campaign. Some examples are shown below.

Situation

An earthquake has destroyed dozens of homes.

Response–donation of goods

People donate clothes, food, toys, bedding, and other household products to those who are now homeless.

Situation

A drought has dried up a local river near several African villages. Now there is no water near the villages.

Response–donation of services

Businesses send equipment and workers at no cost to dig wells near the villages.

Situation

A school wants to raise money to buy new computers. The school decides to put on a fair.

Response–donation of goods

People donate items that can be sold at the fair, such as cakes, toys, and secondhand books.

Fairs are a popular method of fund-raising.

Reasons for fund-raising

People always have a reason for fund-raising. Many people who raise funds feel very strongly about the charity, cause, event, or project they are supporting. Here are some of the most common reasons for fund-raising.

Money for research

Fund-raising can help to pay for **research** into many subjects. This include diseases, pollution, and the protection of endangered animals in their natural environment. Researchers study a subject closely to get information. The information can then be used to make changes that improve lives. Research into some subjects can take many years.

Example   Funds for cancer research

Some scientists want to carry out research into a type of cancer. The scientists want to learn more about the cancer, and how it can be prevented or treated. Money from a fund-raising campaign is used to pay the scientists' **salaries**, and to pay for the materials and equipment they need to do their work.

Fund-raising can help to pay for research.

Money for support

Fund-raising can help to support people and animals in direct need. Support can also be given to improve the lives of people and animals who are not in direct need.

> **Example**   **Funds for people in direct need**
>
> A charity wants to support the victims of a **famine**. Money from a fund-raising campaign is used to pay for food, water, blankets, tents, and medicine for the victims.

Money for protection

Fund-raising can help to pay for projects that protect living things and places from being harmed or destroyed.

> **Example**   **Funds for protecting bears**
>
> An animal **welfare** organization wants to protect bears from cruelty. The bears are kept in cages and milked for their bile, a liquid made inside their livers that is used in traditional medicine. Money from a fund-raising campaign is used to send people to bear farms in Asia. There they get information and photographs, educate people about the issue, and send letters and emails of protest to Asian governments.

Money raised from a fund-raising campaign can be used to educate people about important issues, such as animal welfare.

Money for improvements

Fund-raising can help to pay for improvements to buildings, streets, parks, and other places.

> **Example** **Funds for a new hospital wing**
>
> A hospital wants to build a new children's wing. Money from a fund-raising campaign is used to pay for the cost of the building, furniture, and medical equipment.

Money for maintenance

Fund-raising can help to pay for the maintenance of some places. Maintenance can include cleaning, repairing, painting, and gardening.

> **Example** **Funds for painting a scout hall**
>
> A local scout hall needs painting. Money from a fund-raising campaign is used to pay for the paint and brushes.

Money for the arts

Fund-raising can help to pay for events and projects to do with the arts, such as music, dancing, writing, acting, and painting. Events and projects can include performances, festivals, tours, classes, equipment, and materials.

> **Example** **Funds for staging a play**
>
> A local theater group wants to put on a play. Money from a fund-raising campaign is used to pay for the costumes, the sets, the hire of a hall, and the printing of programs and posters.

Fund-raising money can help a local theater group put on a play.

Convincing people to donate

For fund-raising to work, fund-raisers must convince other people that there is a good reason to give money. This is not always easy. People are asked to donate to many charities, causes, events, and projects, but most people can afford to donate only a small amount of money each year. This means people have to say no to some requests for donations.

Fund-raisers find it is easier to raise funds for some charities, causes, events, and projects than for others. It is usually easier to raise money to help sick or orphaned children than it is to raise money to help people who are homeless or addicted to drugs. Well-known charities have more chance of getting donations than lesser-known charities, because people tend to trust a charity more if they have heard of it. People are more likely to donate to a local event or project if they believe in it, or if it benefits them, their family, or friends.

Well-known charities, such as Save the Children, often have a better chance of raising donations than those that are not as well known.

SAVE THE CHILDREN

Methods of fund-raising

There are many different methods of fund-raising. Some methods are simple and cheap to set up and operate. Other methods require a lot of planning, money, and people.

Simple methods

If a local club, school, or group wants to raise funds, it can use one of the following methods:

- A chocolate drive. Fund-raisers buy chocolate bars at a low price, then make money by selling the bars for a higher price
- A fair. Fund-raisers set up a fair in a school ground or local park. People donate goods, which are sold at stalls. Many fairs also have rides and other forms of entertainment that people pay to use
- A raffle. Fund-raisers offer valuable items, which are often donated, as prizes in a lottery. People buy numbered tickets. The winning tickets are drawn on a set date

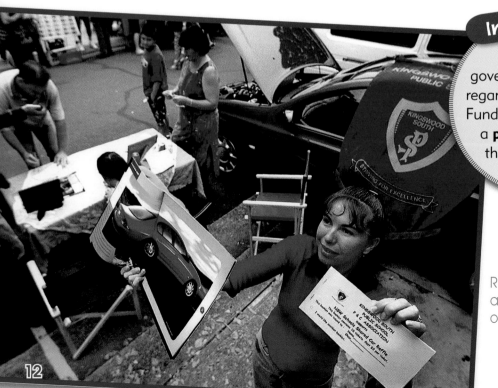

Info-plus!

The government has rules regarding fund-raising. Fund-raisers may need a **permit** to put on their fund-raising activity.

Raffles are a simple and popular method of raising funds.

More complex methods

Large charities or other large organizations may raise funds by using one of the following methods:

- A charity shop. Fund-raisers set up and run a shop that sells donated products. The people who work in the shop are usually volunteers, but the shop's rent and other costs, such as electricity, must still be paid

- Cold calling or mailing. Fund-raisers telephone or send letters to thousands of people at home and work, asking them to donate money

- Collection tins. Fund-raisers holding labelled collection tins stand in public places or knock on people's front doors. The fund-raisers ask people to drop money into the tins

- A telethon. Fund-raisers put on a day-long television program and ask people to telephone in and make donations. The program includes famous people, entertainment, and information about the charity or cause

Info-plus!

Fund-raisers must sometimes spend money to run a fund-raising campaign. This money is deducted, or taken away, from the money raised.

Charity shops sell a variety of donated products.

What are charities?

Charities are organizations set up to assist people and animals who need help. Charities rely on fund-raising to collect money, products, and services. Few charities simply give the money to people. Most charities use the money to provide other types of help, such as food, blankets, medical treatment, and equipment. Charities may also help to fund job-training programs, as well as new hospitals, schools, and animal sanctuaries.

Educating people

Many charities use some of the money they raise to educate people about their work. They do this because people are more likely to give donations if they know what a charity does. By educating people about important issues, charities also hope to persuade them to think and act differently. An animal-rights charity may try to educate people about wild animals being killed for their fur, in the hope that people will not buy fur products.

Many charities, such as People for the Ethical Treatment of Animals, try to educate people about their work.

Médecins sans Frontières is a charity that gives medical aid to people in need.

The work of charities

Charities are set up with a purpose. This purpose is always to benefit and help others, but there are many ways to do this. Most charities work in one or more of the following areas – **humanitarian aid**, human welfare, health, education, the environment, animal welfare, the arts, and religion.

Some charities are set up to provide help in a particular emergency, or to a group or project in one place or country. Other charities work on many different issues, in many different places.

The law

By law, only some organizations can operate as charities. A charity must be not-for-profit. This means that a charity must not raise funds to benefit its members or volunteers. People who are employed by a charity, such as doctors and accountants, can be paid for doing their jobs.

Volunteers

Volunteers are people who offer to do unpaid work. Most fund-raising could not be done without volunteers. If everyone who worked in fund-raising had to be paid, there would be little money left.

Jobs for volunteers

Volunteers do many different fund-raising jobs. They sell raffle tickets and products such as chocolate bars. They run fairs and functions. Volunteers also do office work, and answer telephones during telethons. Some volunteers have special skills that they use to raise funds or save money for the charity. A writer may volunteer to write posters and brochures that publicize a fund-raising activity. An accountant may volunteer to keep a record of all the money received and spent during a fund-raising campaign.

Charities rely on the work done by volunteers.

Working hours

Some volunteers work on a regular basis. A volunteer may work two days a week in a charity's shop, at an animal shelter or in a charity's office. Other volunteers offer their services for a short time during an emergency. A volunteer may work for several days helping to collect money and goods for people affected by a bushfire or earthquake.

Children as volunteers

Children can work as volunteers. They can help adults with fund-raising activities, such as selling raffle tickets. A child can raise money by entering a **walkathon** or **readathon**. Children can also help with many other jobs, such as making posters and setting up stalls.

Children can volunteer to help by entering a fun run to help raise money.

Info-plus!

Some fund-raisers are paid workers. Professional fund-raisers often work on large fund-raising campaigns. They have the knowledge and time, and know the right people, to make the campaign successful.

The role of the media

The media includes television, radio, newspapers, magazines, and the Internet. It is an important daily source of information for most people. Because of this, the media often plays an important role in telling people about fund-raising for charities, causes, events, and projects.

Informing the media

Fund-raisers give details of their fund-raising campaigns to the media, in the hope that the media will tell people about them. The media runs stories on campaigns that it believes are important and will interest people. Many large fund-raising campaigns get a lot of media attention.

Media interviews are a good way for charities, such as Greenpeace, to get their message to many people.

Info-plus!

Many charities have their own Web sites. A charity's Web site contains information about the charity and its work. It explains how to donate money, and how donations are used.

Campaigns in the media

Some fund-raising campaigns are run almost entirely in the media. Telethons are a good example, because they are run on television. Other fund-raising events, such as rock concerts, can be shown on television and the Internet, and played on radio. Telephone numbers are given out during the event so that people can call and make donations. Sometimes the media will advertise campaigns for free. Some famous people will promote fund-raising activities for free.

Big business

Some businesses donate large amounts of money to fund-raising campaigns. Many businesses like the public to know about their donations, because it is good publicity for the business. It also helps to make a business look good. For this reason, some businesses make their donations on telethons and other television or radio programs, or in front of journalists who will write about the donations in newspapers and magazines.

The media will often report stories of large donations made to fund-raising campaigns.

Local fund-raising

Some fund-raising campaigns are run at a local level. People in a local community may be asked to donate funds to a local fund-raising campaign for a family in direct need.

Example — **"Help the Robinsons" campaign**

A few months ago, the Robinson family lived in a three-bedroom house in a country town. One Saturday night, their house burned down. The family of five and their dog escaped unharmed, but everything they owned was destroyed in the fire.

The family did not have any **insurance**, so they did not have any money to rebuild their house or to replace all the things they lost. A local community group started a fund-raising campaign called "Help the Robinsons."

The fund-raisers wanted to raise enough money to pay for:

- a new house
- food
- clothes
- furniture
- books
- toys
- a dog kennel

The fund-raising campaign

The fund-raisers started the campaign by asking the local newspaper and radio station to run stories about it. The stories included information on how and where people could donate money. The fund-raisers also put up posters around town, and held a meeting in the town hall to let people know how they could help. Local shops and the town bank agreed to collect donations.

The results

As a result of the campaign, the Robinsons were offered a small house to live in, rent-free, until their new house was built. People donated clothes, food, furniture, toys, and books, as well as money. A local pet store donated a kennel for the dog. The money raised by the campaign was enough to buy building materials for the new house. Local tradespeople offered to build the house for free on the Robinsons' land.

One year after the fire, the Robinsons moved into their new house.

National fund-raising

Some fund-raising campaigns are run at a national level, and people around the country are asked to make donations or buy products. Here is information about a national non-profit organization, Girl Scouts of the USA, and one of its fund-raising activities.

Girl Scouts of the USA

Girl Scouts of the USA is an organization just for girls. Members go to regular meetings run by adult volunteers. They take part in a variety of activities, such as field trips, sports clinics, and community service projects. The girls have fun, make friends, and develop qualities such as leadership skills, strong values, and self-confidence.

The first Girl Scout troop began in Savannah, Georgia, in 1912. It had 18 members. Today, Girls Scouts of the USA has 2.7 million girl members. There are also 928,000 adult members, who work mainly as volunteers.

Girl Scouts participate in many community events across the United States.

How Girl Scouts of the USA raises funds

To help fund its activities, Girl Scouts of the USA runs numerous fund-raising events every year. Girls in local troops take part in the planning and running of events in their area. Girls Scouts may raise money by:

- selling Girl Scout Cookies®
- walking pets for a fee
- washing cars for a fee
- offering childcare at local events for a fee
- offering face-painting at local events for a fee
- picking up litter after local events for a fee
- making and selling cards for special occasions

Girl Scouts plan how they will sell their cookies.

23

Girl Scout Cookies®

Every year, Girls Scouts sell specially baked cookies to raise funds for the Girl Scout program in their area. Several different varieties of Girl Scout Cookies® are sold.

The cookies are made in bakeries that have been given special licenses by Girl Scouts of the USA. The cookies are sold in boxes.

Girl Scouts sell the cookies by taking orders from friends, neighbors, and local businesses. Some Girl Scouts even set up their own cookie stalls at community events.

Info-plus!

Girl Scouts usually sell cookies between January and April.

Girl Scout Cookies® show photos of Girl Scouts on the boxes.

24

The results

Many people in the United States buy Girl Scout Cookies® every year. The cookies look, smell, and taste good, and they are made in the United States with ingredients from the United States.

Some Girl Scouts are very good salespeople and can sell more than 1,000 boxes of cookies each year. Around 70 percent of the money that each troop raises goes directly to the local Girl Scout council and to the troop. The rest of the money is used to pay the bakers who baked the cookies.

Using the money

Fund-raising through activities such as selling cookies allows Girl Scouts of the USA to continue its work in helping girls develop physically, mentally, and spiritually.

The money raised from cookie sales helps to pay for many Girl Scouting activities.

Info-plus!

More than 400 people work at the Girl Scouts of the USA headquarters in New York City.

25

International fund-raising

Some fund-raising campaigns are run at an international level, and people around the world are asked to make donations. Here is information about an international charity, the Red Cross, and one of its fund-raising appeals.

The Red Cross

The Red Cross is an international humanitarian organization. It aims to provide help to all people in need, including survivors of wars and natural disasters. The Red Cross also provides aid to communities who are not in direct need but may become so. It does this through services and programs such as blood-donation programs and first-aid classes.

The Red Cross relies on donations to do its work. Donations are accepted at all times, but special fund-raising appeals are set up at times when money is desperately needed. This may occur after a natural disaster, such as the Indian Ocean tsunami of 2004.

Info-plus!

In some countries, the Red Cross is called the Red Crescent. This is because a crescent is used instead of a cross as a symbol of the organization in some non-Christian countries.

These children have been helped by the Red Cross, which has given them food to take to their families.

Fund-raising after the Indian Ocean tsunami in 2004

On December 26, 2004, a massive earthquake under the Indian Ocean set off a series of huge waves called a tsunami. The tsunami hit the coasts of many countries in Southeast Asia, and traveled as far as the east coast of Africa. The waves were small at sea, but got larger as they moved closer to the coast. Some were 33 feet (10 m) high when they hit the shore.

The waves crashed onto the land, sweeping away buildings and vehicles. Entire towns and villages were destroyed, and more than 200,000 people died. Many people were injured, and more than a million people were left homeless.

The most deaths and the worst damage occurred in Indonesia, but other countries, such as Sri Lanka, were also badly affected.

The 2004 tsunami destroyed towns and villages across Southeast Asia.

Helping the victims

When the Red Cross learned of the earthquake and tsunami, staff and volunteers began organizing ways of helping the survivors of the disaster. The Red Cross immediately began providing emergency assistance. It also launched an appeal for money.

The media around the world supported the Red Cross appeal, as well as the appeals of many other aid organisations. There were stories about the disaster and the appeal in newspapers and magazines, as well as on the television, radio, and Internet. Special fund-raising concerts were broadcast in the media. There were telethons and other media activities.

Many individuals, clubs, schools, and businesses also set up their own fund-raising events, and gave the money raised to the Red Cross appeal.

The Red Cross sent desperately needed supplies to the areas affected by the tsunami.

Info-plus!

Many aid organizations raised funds to help survivors of the tsunami. The organizations often worked together, and continue to work together, to provide the survivors with the best help possible.

The results

The Red Cross fund-raising appeal was very successful. The American Red Cross alone raised more than $568 million. Some of this money was used to provide immediate help to the survivors. Some of it will be used to pay for long-term projects in the affected areas, such as building houses.

Using the money

Some of the money raised by the Red Cross appeal was used in the following ways:

- to send skilled people, such as doctors, to the affected areas
- to give medical treatment to injured and sick people
- to provide people with clean water
- to buy and hand out food, clothing, blankets, and household products
- to help bring together families separated during the disaster
- to provide tents and shelter to survivors
- to help people identify bodies

Info-plus!

One year after the disaster, the American Red Cross and its partners had provided help to more than 30 million people living in tsunami-affected countries.

A Red Cross team takes a water-purification unit to a tsunami-affected area in Sri Lanka.

Raise funds for your school

You can raise funds for your school by running an art auction.
Get permission from your parents and teachers before you begin.

You will need:

- pieces of art created and donated by the students
- a computer
- paper
- a printer
- a cash box

Hill Parade High School
Student art auction!
February 25,
7 p.m. in the school gym
32 Hill Parade Summerville

What to do before the auction

1 Choose a date and time for the art auction.
2 Use your computer, printer, and paper to make posters advertizing the auction to potential buyers.
3 Put the posters up in your local area.
4 Put information about the auction in your school newsletter.
5 Contact your local newspaper and ask them to do a story on the auction.

What to do on the day of the auction

1 Display the art. Give each piece a number.
2 Put out chairs for the bidders.
3 Get your principal to auction each piece by number.
4 Take the money from each sale and put it in a cash box.
5 After the auction, count the money and present it to your principal.

Glossary

auctioned when an item is sold to the person who offers the most money

bequests money or property that a person leaves in their will to another person or organization

campaigns series of planned activities for specific purposes

cause an issue that some people believe in strongly

donations gifts of money, products, or services

famine an extreme shortage of food in an area

humanitarian aid providing help to large numbers of people, to reduce their suffering and improve their wellbeing

insurance an agreement with a business that promises to pay you money if you are hurt or lose products

permit a written order giving permission to do something

products objects that are bought, sold, or bartered

readathon a form of fund-raising where the participants receive donations according to the number of books read

rehabilitate to help return to good health and normal activities

research the study of a subject to get information

salaries set amounts of money that are paid regularly to employees for their work

services work that people pay others to do or provide

volunteers people who offer to do unpaid work

walkathon a form of fund-raising where the participants receive donations according to the distance walked

welfare well-being

Index